WORMOLOGY

WORMOLOGY

by Michael Elsohn Ross

photographs by Brian Grogan • illustrations by Darren Erickson

Carolrhoda Books, Inc. / Minneapolis

To my sisters, Cathy and Jody, who used to play with worms, too.

Without the creativity and enthusiasm of the second through sixth grade students of El Portal Elementary and the support of their teachers, Carl Brownless and Phyllis Weber, this book would not have been possible. I would also like to thank the students of Vista de Valle School in Claremont, California, and Tom Jones and his students at Alicia Reyes School in Merced, California, for their assistance.

Text copyright © 1996 by Michael Elsohn Ross
Photographs copyright © 1996 by Brian Grogan
Illustrations copyright © 1996 by Carolrhoda Books, Inc.

Carolrhoda Books, Inc. c/o The Lerner Group
241 First Avenue North, Minneapolis, MN 55401

LIBRARY OF CONGRESS CATALOGING-IN-PUBLICATIONS DATA

Ross, Michael Elsohn
    Wormology / by Michael Elsohn Ross ; photographs by Brian Grogan ;
illustrated by Darren Erickson.
        p.   cm. — (Backyard buddies)
    Includes index.
    ISBN 0-8614-937-9
    1. Earthworm—Juvenile literature. 2. Earthworms—Experiments—Juvenile literature.
[1. Earthworms.] I. Grogan, Brian, ill. II. Erickson, Darren, ill. III. Title. IV. Series: Ross, Michael Elsohn, Backyard buddies
QL391.A6R67 1995
595.1'46—dc20   94-42435
                                                                        CIP
                                                                        AC

Manufactured in the United States of America
1 2 3 4 5 6 - JR - 01 00 99 98 97 96

Contents

Would you wiggle through dirt

without pants or shirt?

Would you eat your own path

and never take a bath?

Would you take a turn

as an earthworm?

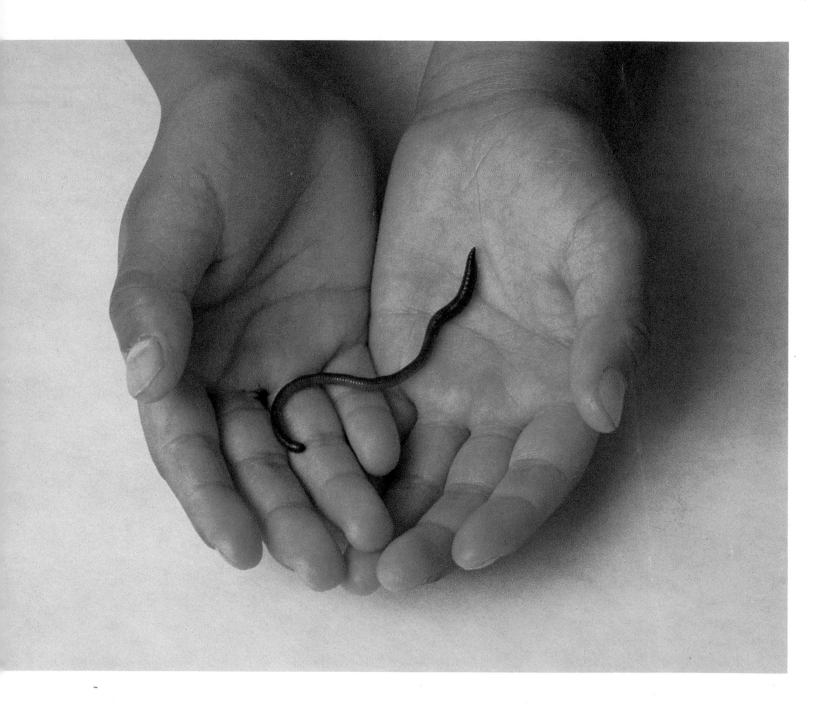

No doubt you have seen one of these before. In fact, you may have dug one up while poking about in the dirt. Perhaps you've even picked one up and let it wiggle in your hands.

Welcome to Wormology

Nicknamed "worms" by most folks, these creatures are more precisely known as earthworms. Though most of them live in the earth, they are also found under leaf piles, tree bark, manure, and even in water.

Some people are frightened by earthworms. Other folks may think of them as mere fish bait, but earthworms are neighbors worth getting to know. Even though we share backyards, their lives are very different from ours. So different, in fact, that you could imagine they lived on another planet.

Anthropologists are explorers who learn about their human neighbors by observing people's actions. Wormologists are adventurers who learn about their earthworm neighbors by watching worms. They are also scientists who study living things with care and concern for the lives of small creatures. To practice wormology you do not need to hurt or kill anything. The gentler you are, the more successful you'll be. All you need is plenty of curiosity and a touch of patience.

Are you ready to worm your way into wormology? Just keep reading and you'll be on the trail.

If you live in the city, desert, or where there's not much soil, you may have to buy some earthworms from a bait shop or plant nursery. But if there's a lawn, garden, meadow, or woods nearby, then it's time for a worm hunt. All you will need is a small container with a lid, and a trowel or shovel. It's a good idea to get permission before you start digging in some special place, like your neighbor's prize flower garden.

Earthworms love moist, rotten places. That is, they like any damp spot where there are rotting

Casting for Worms

leaves, fruit, or other stuff. You'll know you're hot on the trail if you find little crumbly piles of dirt that look like they were squeezed from tiny toothpaste tubes. These deposits are called **castings.** They are cast off by earthworms as they munch their way through the soil.

Gently dig under the castings. When you find an earthworm, simply drop it into your container with some soil and moist leaves. If the worm is partly underground, gently loosen the soil around it until it falls out. Worms live in underground

tunnels called **burrows.** They can anchor themselves in their burrows by gripping the walls with small bristles, called **setae** (SEE-tee), and by puffing out their bodies until they fit tight like a cork in a bottle. Their grip is so strong that they'll break before they lose hold. Do not pull on a worm that is still in its burrow—it might break in two.

At night when worms are active, you can use a flashlight to search for ones that might be poking out of their underground burrows. Worms also come out when it rains—this is another great time to search the ground for worms.

Keep your new friends in the shade. Direct sunlight can be deadly to these creatures of the underworld! And handle them with care. Just because you're bigger doesn't mean you can't be gentle. Earthworms, like all living things, deserve respect.

setae

Before you introduce the worms to your household, consider how your folks will react. If they are people who freak out about crawly critters, you can assure them that worms are better than most pets. Tell them, "Worms don't bite, eat pet food, or need shots. They don't bark, tear up the carpet, or devour slippers. They're so quiet inside a jar of dirt, you'll hardly even know they're there. Now, do you want me to pester you for a boa constrictor or will you let me keep the worms?"

Dogs and cats aren't very happy when they are kept in the cupboard or closet, but worms don't mind small, dark places. In fact, a jar full of soil is like a palace to an earthworm. With walls and ceilings of lovely damp dirt, your underground guests will feel like royalty. If you would like to make a worm palace, just check out the instructions below and on the next page.

Underground Palace

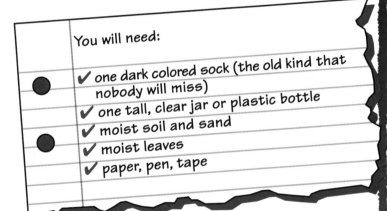

You will need:

- ✔ one dark colored sock (the old kind that nobody will miss)
- ✔ one tall, clear jar or plastic bottle
- ✔ moist soil and sand
- ✔ moist leaves
- ✔ paper, pen, tape

Palace Construction:

1. Fill the jar one-third full of moist soil. The soil should feel damp, but not soggy. If you are using a tall, clear plastic bottle with a skinny top, such as the type window-washing fluid comes in, ask an adult to help you cut the skinny top off before adding soil.

2. Add a one-inch layer of sand and then fill to within two inches of the top with more soil.

3. Top off with a delicious layer of moist, decaying leaves.

4. Drop in a few earthworms and pull the sock over the entire palace. The sock will keep the palace dark and allow the worms to tunnel up against the walls of the container, where you may be able to see them later when you remove the sock.

5. Make a sign that tells who lives inside. It's a good idea to warn any new guests to your house about your worm friends.

6. Keep the palace in a dark cupboard or closet. Your worms will need a chance to relax, so hang up a "Do Not Disturb" sign and leave them alone for a day.

Not everyone will think your jar of worms is a palace, so it's important that your palace has a guard—you. A guard keeps an eye on royalty and protects them from harm. You need to make sure the soil is damp and leaves are available. Add a tablespoon of water and a fresh supply of leaves at least once a week.

While you have the sock off, you can also look for worms. Those that burrowed down along the

Palace Guard

sides of the jar might be in clear view. Do you see any worms or burrows? Check out the layers of soil. Did any worms tunnel through? How did the worms react when you took the sock off?

Most people probably don't think there's anything to learn from watching a jar of dirt. They don't know what they're missing! A jar of dirt is full of mysteries and entertainment.

Life in a palace can get a little boring, even for royal worms. Be an entertaining host and create a play park for your earthworms.

Gently touch it. What does it feel like? What does it do?

For even more fun, add a few extra worms to the play park. What do you think will happen?

Have you ever thought of yourself as an enormous jungle gym? To become one, all you need to do is place a worm on your hand. Sit still and watch. Can it climb up your arm? Over your arm hairs? Does it tickle?

When playtime is over, be sure to return the worms to their palace. They'll be safer there than sliming their way across the floor.

You will need:

- ✔ a large baking pan (with the cook's permission)
- ✔ a handful of dirt
- ✔ a small container of water
- ✔ toys, such as balls, minicars, or blocks
- ✔ a handful of old, moist leaves
- ✔ anything else you can think of

Place an earthworm in the play park. What do you think it will do? Watch it for a while. What happens? Does it spend more time at one piece of playground equipment than another?

Now pretend you're a giant that comes upon the park. (You really are a giant, aren't you?) Very quietly sneak up close to the worm and peer at it. Does it seem to notice you? How can you tell?

Are you aware? Would you notice if your mom frizzed her hair and dyed it purple? Would you notice if your teacher wore a new pair of shoes? Are you tuned in to small details? Whatever your answers, the Aware Dare is for you. If you are totally oblivious (that means out to lunch), then this game will help you focus on the little stuff. Such focusing comes in handy, especially when you are getting acquainted with new creatures, such as earthworms. If you are totally tuned in, this game will give you a chance to show off your remarkable talents. Though it can be played alone, the Aware Dare is wilder with two or more players.

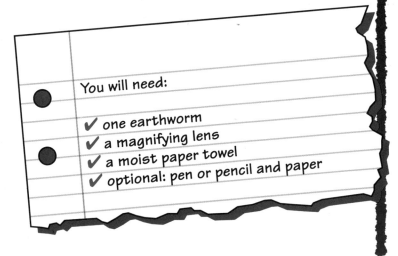

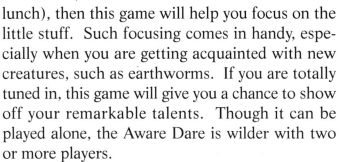

You will need:

✔ one earthworm
✔ a magnifying lens
✔ a moist paper towel
✔ optional: pen or pencil and paper

How to Play:

1. Decide on the order of play.

Optional: pick one player to write down what each of you notices.

2. Place the worm on the moist paper towel and scrutinize it. (That means, look at it with detective eyes.)

3. Beginning with player number one, take turns sharing observations about the worm. For example, "I notice that it wiggles," or "It is the color of silly putty." Any observation is okay, but no repeats are allowed. However, more details can be added to someone else's observation. For example, though someone may have said, "It wiggles," another person can say, "It wiggles when it is touched."

4. Continue taking turns in the same order until only one player is able to make a new observation. The last person to share a wormy detail is the champion observer.

Worm Computers

Have you ever seen a dog with six legs, a turtle with a square shell, or a cat with a three-foot-long tail? If you have, you probably noticed it immediately, because our brains are constantly on the alert for oddities. Like computers, they compare new data with what is stored in memory. When something doesn't make sense, a little signal goes off, and we begin to wonder. Are you ready to scan the local earthworms with your very personal computer?

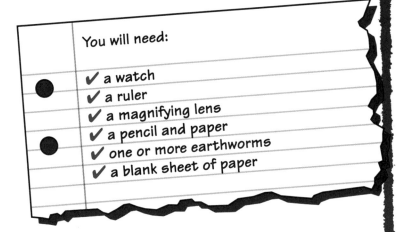

You will need:

- ✔ a watch
- ✔ a ruler
- ✔ a magnifying lens
- ✔ a pencil and paper
- ✔ one or more earthworms
- ✔ a blank sheet of paper

Use the tools and materials listed to examine your worms.

Length: How long are worms? How long is your longest worm? Do you notice how your worm stretches when it moves? How long does it stretch? How short is it when it pulls back in?

Speed: How fast are worms? Time a worm to see how fast it can crawl off a sheet of paper. Can you find another worm that can break the speed record?

Parts: How many different kinds of parts can you see? What do they look like? Are there ears, armpits, or toenails? Are the parts in different shapes? How many shapes can you see?

Rings: How many rings does a worm have? Peer through a magnifying lens, use a blade of grass for a pointer, and see if you can count them. It could be the challenge of a lifetime or just a good excuse for not doing your chores. "Gee, Dad, I can't interrupt my earthworm studies at a time like this!" Good luck and happy computing.

Imagine waking from a deep sleep to a strange hissing sound. Outside the window you spy an immense, glowing, alien spacecraft. After emitting a cloud of green vapors, a hatch slides open. Out wiggles an enormous pinkish brown creature, expanding and contracting like a living accordion. Is this a dream or is this the arrival of the space worm?

Meet a Space Worm

right next to it. Draw what you see. Remember that when you are standing next to it, you can only see parts of it, so draw just the parts of the worm you see. To make the worm look like a giant, include parts of the toys in these close-up views.

Now pretend you are hovering in a helicopter, just above the giant worm. Draw what you see (including the toys). Fly higher and sketch some of the different shapes it makes as it moves. Now go show the drawings to your folks. But before they get scared and move out of town, let them know it's just another wormology fantasy.

You will need:

✔ a magnifying lens
✔ a pencil or pen
✔ blank paper
✔ small toy people or cars

Nab a magnifying lens and examine a worm. For fun, place some small cars or miniature toy people next to it. Pretend it's a giant space worm and that you are standing

Wondertime

Do you wonder about earthworms? Some kids in my town did. Here are some of their questions:

Which end is their head on? Do they have eyes? Do they have brains? Muscles? Intestines?

Do worms have three hearts?

How do they move? Can they climb? Can they hear? Can they swim? Can they crawl upside down?

What do they eat?

Do worms float? How long can worms stay underwater? Do they have to come up for a breath?

How do worms breathe? Can they breathe in the dirt? Can they communicate?

How long does it take a worm to get underground? Why do they live underground?

How do they mate? Do they lay eggs?

Did they have hair when they were babies?

How old can they get?

How big is the biggest worm? How many kinds are there?

Can worms go through a maze?

Do you have any answers for these questions? Do you have any questions of your own? If you do, don't let them escape! Most great explorations started with wondering. For example, think about the folks who may have asked, "What is it like at the North Pole?" or "Is it possible to sail around the world?" Those who followed their curiosity most likely had some outrageous adventures. Consider chasing some of your own personal ponderings. Who knows, you could end up on some crazy journeys, too!

Are you ready for a wild and crazy challenge? If you are, all you have to do to get started is focus on a wormy question. Is there something you really wonder about earthworms? Yes? Well, follow that question. The tips below may help you stay hot on the trail.

Follow That Question

—**Experiment:** Experimentation is one road to discovery. Check out the Kid Experiments section on page 34 to get some ideas of how other people learned more about earthworms. Perhaps you too can design an experiment to explore your questions.

—**Scrutinize:** Do you think you could answer your question if you did a little more observation? For example, if your question was, "Do they have eyes?" do you think you might be able to find the answer if you examined a worm closely through a magnifying lens?

—**Find an Expert:** Do you know any people who know a lot about bugs and other little creatures? A local gardener, agriculture teacher, or verniculturalist (a worm farmer) may be able to help. The answer may be only a phone call away.

—**Research:** Other wormologists may have asked your question in the past and discovered an answer. Perhaps you could check out some books. In fact, a great book to refer to is this one. Turn the page and search through the next section. If that doesn't work, come back to this page and read on.

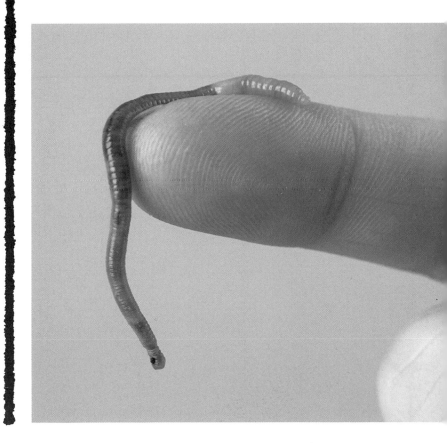

Check out this worm poster. Can you find eyes, a nose, arms, legs, antennae, or teeth?

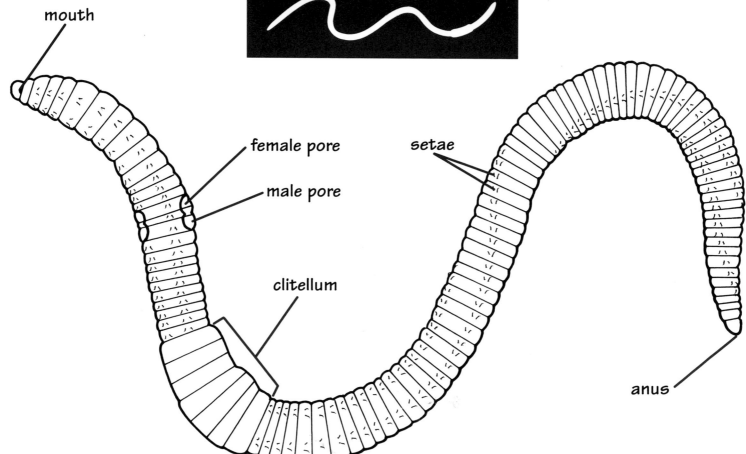

mouth

female pore

male pore

setae

clitellum

anus

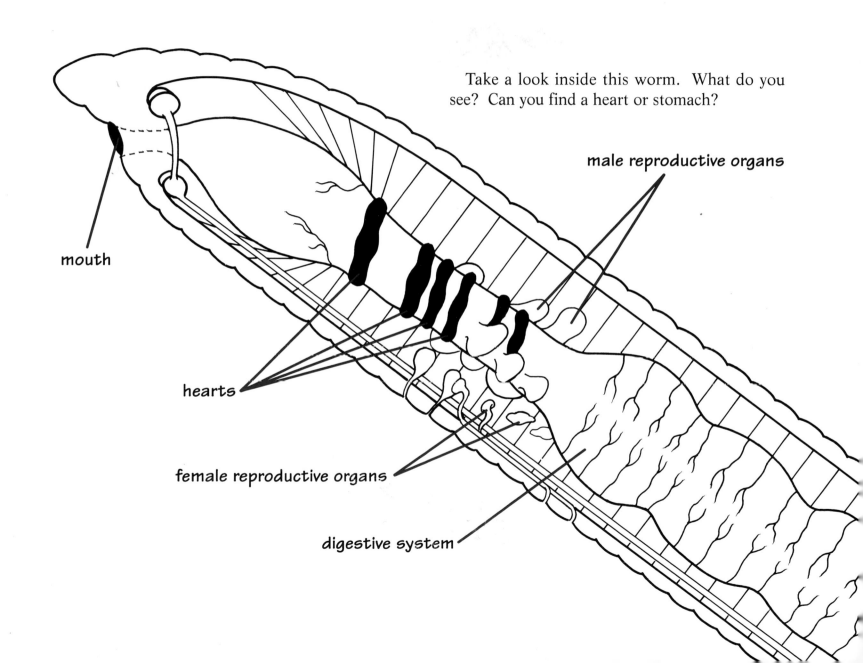

Take a look inside this worm. What do you see? Can you find a heart or stomach?

male reproductive organs

mouth

hearts

female reproductive organs

digestive system

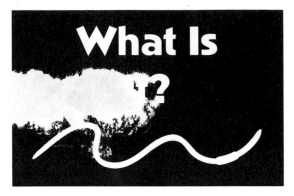

What Is

Earthworms aren't the only creatures called worms. There are tapeworms and pinworms, flatworms and roundworms, mealworms and heartworms, even glowworms, but none these are related to the earthworm. None of these are segmented worms. The rings (segments) on an earthworm distinguish it as a **segmented worm** or **annelid** (AN-uh-lid).

Segmented worms have been on Earth a long time. Their remains have been found in rocks formed in ancient oceans 650 million years ago. That's way before insects, dinosaurs, birds, or bunnies were around.

Many annelids, such as peacock and feather-duster worms, still make the ocean their home, while other segmented worms, such as lung-worms, are found along the ocean shore. The bloodsucking leech, another earthworm relative, lives in ponds and streams. Most segmented worms are covered with bristle or hairlike structures, while earthworms are relatively bald.

Perhaps you thought if you'd seen one earthworm you'd seen them all, but nothing could be further from the truth. Wormologists have discovered about 1,800 **species** of earthworms living everywhere but in the coldest and driest parts of the globe. One of the largest is the giant Australian earthworm, which grows as long and as thick as a broom handle. Would you believe it if you saw a worm as fat as a firehose and as long as a bus? That's what a South African newspaper reported in the 1960s! The smallest earthworms, in contrast, are shorter than your thumbnail and skinnier than a toothpick.

Each language has its own names for creatures. Earthworm in Spanish is *lombriz* (lom-BREEZ). In German it is *Regenwurm* (REH-gen-vurm), in Zulu *umsundu,* and in French it is *ver de terre* (VAIR-duh-TAIR). Since all these names can be confusing, scientists have given each species of living things one name. Whether you live in New Zealand or Africa, the scientific name for a plant or animal is the same. These scientific names are in the ancient languages of Latin and Greek.

Did you know most people call dinosaurs by their scientific names? When you say Tyrannosaurus rex, you are saying "terrible lizard king." If you can rattle off the scientific names for dinosaurs, you can certainly say the scientific name of the common earthworm, *Lumbricus* (lum-BREE-kus) *terrestris* (ter-RES-tris). Try saying that three times in a row!

Earthworms are part of the group of segmented worms known as annelids. Annelids are part of a larger group of animals called **invertebrates** (in-VER-tuh-brets). Invertebrates don't have backbones. All the animals below are invertebrates.

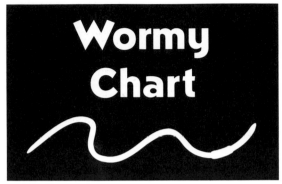

Wormy Chart

Annelids are invertebrate worms with many ringlike segments. (*Annel* is Latin for "ring.") The animals below are all annelids.

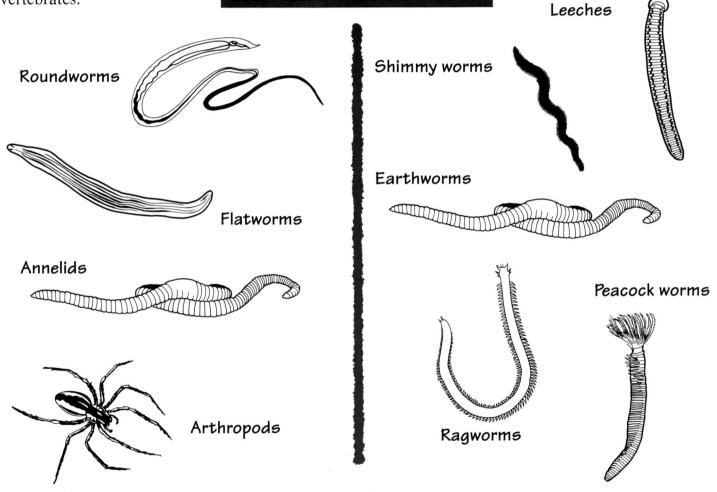

Roundworms

Flatworms

Annelids

Arthropods

Shimmy worms

Earthworms

Leeches

Peacock worms

Ragworms

How is an earthworm like a cowboy's horse?

They both wear saddles, of course.

The earthworm is a special type of annelid that has a saddlelike hump called a **clitellum** (klih-TEH-lum). (*Clitellae* is Latin for "packsaddle.") The leech, a bloodsucking freshwater worm, has suckers on the front and rear, in

addition to having a saddle. Since both leeches and earthworms have saddles, they are both in the group of annelids called Clitellata. Annelids in the group Polychaeta (pah-lee-KEET-uh) live in or near the sea and look like surfboards with hairy paddles. *Polychaeta* is Latin for "many" (*poly*) "bristle" (*chaeta*).

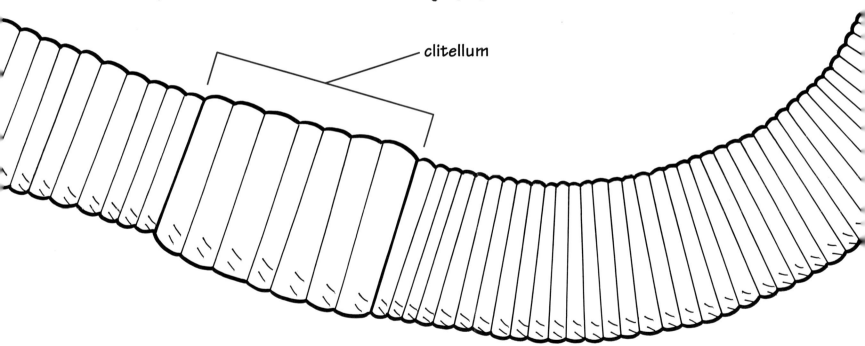

clitellum

How is a worm like a surfer? They both ride waves!

Unlike a surfer, though, a worm rides waves that are inside its body, not underneath it. If you want to see for yourself, all you have to do is take a close look.

traction. Their cleats, or setae, prevent the worm from slipping backward as it stretches. Once the worm is all stretched out, it must squish back together in order to stretch out again. While gripping the ground with its front end, the setae let go and the worm pulls together like an accordion. Since the front end is anchored, the tail of the worm slides forward. Thus, by stretching its front end and pulling in its rear, an earthworm moves ahead in the world.

To go backward, a worm merely reverses the direction of its waves and grips with its tail. See if you can get your worm to switch directions. Check out the waves. Look for the setae with a magnifying lens. You can find them on the underside of the worm. Spy on your worm as it squishes together. Do you see how it grips the ground?

Get down on the floor and try to move without using your arms and legs. Try pulling yourself along with your snout. It's not so easy, is it? (Unless, of course, you're an earthworm.)

You will need:

✔ one earthworm
✔ a damp paper towel
✔ a magnifying lens

Place a worm on a moist paper towel and watch it cruise. Can you see how it gets longer and shorter and longer and shorter and longer and shorter? Watch the rings. Can you see how they move in waves? Starting at the head, the worm stretches each section, one at a time, all the way to the tail. This muscle flexing makes a wave. Like soccer players, worms wear cleats for

A Worm in Motion

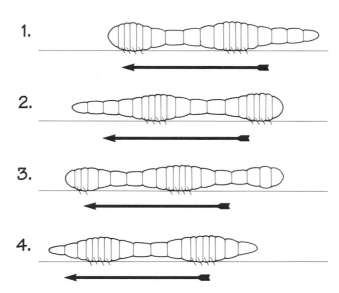

Aristotle, the great scientist of ancient Greece, called earthworms the **intestines** of the Earth. Perhaps he was right. A worm is like a long bag with guts, or intestines, inside. Food enters through the mouth and exits at the other end. As a worm munches dead leaves, plants, and animals, it turns them into casts, which become part of the topsoil. Thus, natural waste is digested, and parts of the earth are recycled.

Without this natural recycling, plants wouldn't have fertilizer and would be unable to grow. And without plants, there would be no food for animals. That's why earthworms and other **scavengers** are important to our survival. Perhaps that's why they are considered the guts of the Earth.

Earthworms are most active at night. While you sleep, as many as twenty thousand may be busily devouring the natural waste in your back-

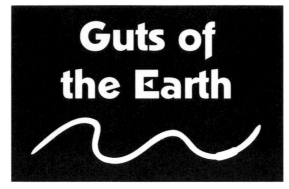

Guts of the Earth

yard. The common earthworm feeds by poking itself partway out of its burrow and using its snout to gather fallen leaves. Other types of worms feed on goodies they find as they nudge through the soil. If the soil is too hard to poke through, worms use another feeding technique. Worms have the remarkable ability to send part of their throats outward, collect dirt with it, and then swallow by popping it back in. Earthworms can actually eat their way through hard-packed soil.

The soil is like a gritty casserole with delicious and nutritious bacteria, fungi, and roundworms mixed in. As worms gobble up the casserole, they also munch these tasty morsels. Though these are the only live beasties that most earthworms eat, some mammoth West African worms have even been known to chow on other earthworms.

Mythical Creatures

Ancient Greeks told many strange tales about the lives of their gods and goddesses. One of the weirdest is the story about Hermaphroditus. When Hermaphroditus was a young man, he took a dip in a beautiful fountain. The nymph who guarded it fell in love with him, but he didn't feel the same way. Since she couldn't bear to see him leave, she used magic to become part of his body. Now Hermaphroditus had both the parts of a man and of a woman. Now he was also a she. Needless to say, he looked and felt quite unusual.

When scientists discovered animals that had both boy and girl parts in one body, they called them **hermaphrodites** (hur-MAF-ro-dytz) in reference to Hermaphroditus. Earthworms are one of these animals. Each worm has both male and female parts. They can be both a mother and a father at the same time. During mating, worms line up to each other in opposite directions and fertilize each other's eggs. Eggs are deposited in hardened **cocoons** made from goop that oozes from each worm's saddle. You can look for these cocoons in the topsoil. They are the size of a rice grain and the shape of a lemon. Some worms may produce over one hundred per year!

Once in the soil, a cocoon can take anywhere from a month to more than a year to hatch. The warmer the soil, the faster the hatching. Even though a cocoon may contain several eggs, most of the time only one will hatch. Baby worms, miniature models of their parents, eat and grow like crazy. Like their parents, baby worms are hairless except for the bristles, their setae, which they use to grip the ground. Within twenty months, they will have grown to twelve times their original length. After only three months, they can mate, lay cocoons of their own, and give birth to more boy/girl worms.

Worms Mating

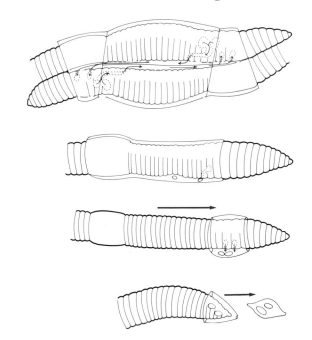

Slimy Breather

Did you know that you and all of your friends are slimy breathers? You can't deny it. Just check out those slimy airholes, your nose and your mouth. They're coated with a slippery, slimy **mucus** that protects us as we breathe. Mucus lets water and air pass in, while gumming up and snagging germs, dust, and other unwanted gunk.

An earthworm does not breathe through nostrils or a mouth, but it's also a slimy breather. Unlike people, worms breathe through their entire skin. Air and water from the soil just pass through a worm's hide and into its blood. A worm needs moisture to keep its skin slimy. If a worm ventures away from damp, shady places, it's in danger of drying out and then suffocating.

Some South American and African earthworms are tail breathers. They live in stagnant swamps where there is little oxygen in the soil. These worms have "lunglike" organs on their rears that allow them to breathe from above the ground, while the rest of their bodies are stuck in muck.

Did you notice how slippery worm slime is? Worms also use their mucus to help them slide over the ground. In fact, worms usually leave a slime track containing a special scent that helps them find their burrows again.

In many parts of the world, there are wet and dry seasons. When the soil begins to dry out, worms must burrow down to find places that are still moist. Since most worm food is in or near the top layer of soil, the deeper they go, the less food there is. They can live on a diet of limited food and water, although they may become slim and a bit parched. When the rains return, worms wiggle upward to fill up with food and drink once again.

Deep burrows also protect worms from below-zero temperatures. Instead of flying south for the winter, most worms living in cold climates simply travel downward and then return to the surface in the spring. In Russia there is a type of worm that is so tough, it doesn't need to escape the cold. It just freezes solid like a popsicle and survives in this rigid state until a thaw allows it to move about again.

Early Bird Feeders

Have you ever heard the saying "The early bird gets the worm"? Well, it's not just early birds who get worms. Mammals such as badgers, foxes, skunks, hedgehogs, and moles find their fair share too! Moles make certain species of earthworms helpless by biting off three to five of their front segments. Gardeners sometimes dig up piles of still living but inactive worms in mole burrows, where they have been stored by the mole for a winter snack. Worms are the main food of baby badgers; foxes will dine on worms when rabbits are scarce; and the long-beaked echidna eats nothing else.

Toads, salamanders, lizards, and snakes will snaffle up worms too. Beetles and mole crickets munch on them. Killer slugs and snails gnaw them. Ants and centipedes will even bite them. In South Africa, giant earthworms are attacked by night adders. (Night adders are poisonous snakes, not kids doing math homework after dinner.) For a worm, an encounter with any of these hungry creatures can be a once-in-a-lifetime experience, but the most dangerous critters are birds. A flock of golden plovers, for example, has been known to gulp down half the worms in a meadow in just three weeks of hunting. Being a worm is not a safe occupation. A worm in the wild is lucky to reach the age of a preschooler. Worms can live to be over ten years old, but usually only in captivity, when protected from danger. Life isn't easy for a critter that tastes so good.

echidna

Chopped Worms

When you live in the dirt, shovels and spades spell trouble with a capital T. Sadly, as many a gardener knows, it's difficult to dig in the soil without chopping worms. And it's nearly impossible not to wonder what will happen to the unlucky victim. Despite what many folks have heard, one worm sliced in half does not make two. Yet something else amazing does occur. Most kinds of earthworms can grow back chopped tails, and a few species can even grow back their front ends. The trick is not to lose too many sections. If too many are lost, so is the poor worm. Five segments is too many for the *Lumbricus terrestris*, the common backyard worm, to lose, but its relative, the dung earthworm, can lose as many as twenty-three.

Unfortunately, even dung worms don't end up as long and lovely as they were before being chopped by a shovel or a hunter's fangs. The closer the break is to the middle, the slimmer the chance that all the cutoff rings will reappear. However, being a bit shorter is a lot better than being someone else's meal.

THUNK!

The kids at my local elementary school in El Portal, California, had plenty of questions that led to some pretty fun experiments.

Do Worms Get Along?

Elizabeth placed several worms together in a container and watched them carefully. They didn't fight, run away, or hiss at each other. "They just climbed over each other," she remarked and decided that they were getting along fine.

What Can Worms Crawl Up?

Mandy placed her worm on different objects to see which ones they could crawl up. She discovered that they could crawl up rulers better than pencils and that they could also climb up chairs. What else do you think they can crawl up?

Would you believe that some earthworms can slither up onto trees and rooftops? That's what one scientist reported observing in Southeast Asia.

Can Worms Swim?

Libby and Jessie placed two cups of water on the table. Into each went a worm. The girls noticed that all the worms sank and squiggled about on the bottom. Neither of the worms could get out of the containers. Libby and Jessie thought they would need something to crawl out on. Can you devise an experiment to see if they were right?

What Happens to a Worm in Water?

Kim tested two worms. She immersed each worm in a cup of water for a full minute before taking it out. She repeated the test three times. While each worm was in the water, Kim observed them and kept notes. Here are her results:

	EXPERIMENT		
	#1	#2	#3
Worm #1	Stayed calm	Didn't struggle, looked confused	Got skinnier, just crawled
Worm #2	Struggled, but didn't die	Crawled as if outside, got skinnier.	Struggled, got skinnier

Do Worms Prefer Soil or Water?

Caitlin and Jessica constructed a maze using small colored blocks to find out. They placed water on one end and soil on the other end. One at a time, they put seven different worms into the maze. Do you think worms prefer soil or water? Check out the results:

Soil	Water	Neither
2	4	1

Do you have any idea why more worms went to the water? Jessica thought they went to the water because they were thirsty.

Do Earthworms Like Vibrations?

Tylar and Aaron set a worm in the middle of a desk and then pounded on the desk to see if the worm would go toward the pounding or away from it. Even though the first worm got bounced by Aaron's enthusiastic pounding, it managed to get a grip on the tabletop and head away from the tablequake. Aaron and Tylar took turns pounding as they tested four more worms. What do you think happened? If you guessed that all the worms hightailed it out of there, you're right.

How Do Worms React to Substances?

GJ wanted to discover how earthworms behaved when they came into contact with different substances that he found in the classroom science cupboard. He began by pouring a small amount of vinegar onto a worm. Unfortunately, the worm died immediately, and GJ decided to devise a method of testing that wouldn't be harmful to the worms. Like many scientists, GJ was following his basic belief that the lives of creatures, both big and small, are something precious. For his new setup, GJ placed three paper towels on the table so they created a triangle in the center. He moistened each towel with a different substance and then one at a time, placed worms in a small puddle of water in the center. This is what happened:

Worm #1	went toward the ammonia.
Worm #2	stayed in the center.
Worm #3	stayed in the center.
Worm #4	went under the towel moistened with ammonia.
Worm #5	withdrew quickly after it went toward the vinegar, did the same with the alcohol, and ended up on the towel with ammonia.

GJ wondered why the worms went to the ammonia. Manure piles and compost heaps often give off ammonia gas. Perhaps the worms went toward the ammonia in hopes of finding a meal.

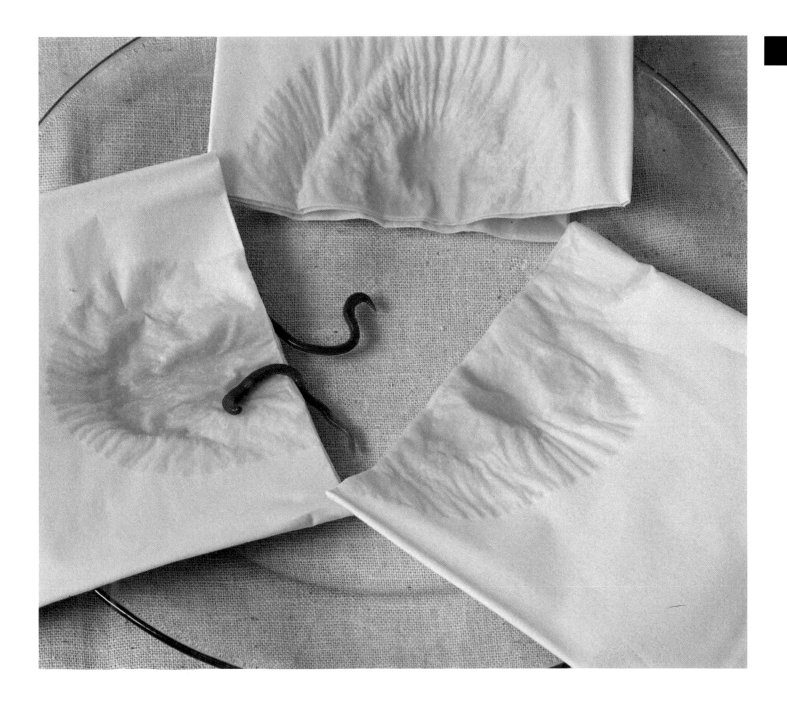

How Far Can a Worm Go in a Minute?

Chelsea and Caitlin set up a worm racetrack with two yardstick walls bordering a dirt track. The legless little racers were placed on the track one at a time. As one girl kept track of time, the other measured the worm's progress by checking the numbers on the yardstick. Here are the results of ten tests:

Though Worm Number Four was the fastest, it was still pretty slow. It would have had to stay at top speed for five minutes to cover one yard. It would take Number Four about three days traveling at top speed to travel a half mile. Most kids can walk that same distance in less than fifteen minutes.

Worm	Distance
#1	1½ inches
#2	1½ inches
#3	2 inches
#4	8 inches
#5	3 inches
#6	½ inch
#7	2½ inches
#8	1¼ inches
#9	6¾ inches

How Fast Can a Worm Burrow?

Carolyn timed her worms burrowing in different kinds of soil. She filled two cups to the brim with sand and two cups with soil. She added two drops of water to each cup. As she placed each worm in a cup, she recorded the time. Below are her results.

—Worms in soil:

Worm #1: Placed on soil at 1:19 P.M. At 1:24 worm began to dig and was fully covered by 1:33 P.M. Total burrowing time: 9 minutes.

Worm #2: Placed on soil at 1:31 P.M. Worm began digging at 1:34 and was covered by 1:41 P.M. Total burrowing time: 7 minutes.

—Worms in sand:

Worm #1: Placed on sand at 1:21 P.M. Worm tried to crawl out of the cup, so some sand was removed. Began digging at 1:24 and was covered by 1:35 P.M. Total burrowing time: 11 minutes.

Worm #2: Placed on sand at 1:30 P.M. By 1:50 worm was still not under, and it was time for the spelling quiz.

In the 1800s Charles Darwin, whom you can learn more about on the next page, timed the burrowing of a large worm in hard-packed wet sand. Would you believe it took twenty-five hours and forty minutes for the worm to tunnel under?

Did you know wormology can lead to greatness? Charles Darwin, one of the greatest scientists of all time, was a devoted wormologist. In fact, he investigated earthworms for over forty years and published a book about them when he was seventy-two years old. His studies of worms, corals, orchids, barnacles, and other living things provided the basis for his theory of evolution. Evolution explains how living things change over long periods of time.

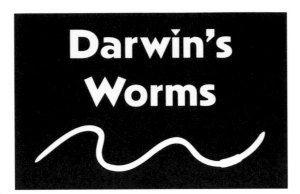

Worms were the perfect creature to study. Not only did they live in Darwin's backyard, they were also easy and exciting to experiment with. As Darwin studied these lowly worms, he discovered that they were more complex and special than they had first seemed.

Light Experiments

Since Darwin knew that worms were creatures of the night, he was curious about how they would react to light. To find out, he set up a series of experiments. The worms were housed in pots, and all of the experiments were done at night when the worms were out of their burrows. Darwin figured that the less disturbance he made, the more successful his experiments would be, so he always crept up quietly to the worm pots.

In his first light test, he shined a red light on the pots, and the worms showed no reaction at all. However, when he illuminated the pots with a regular lamp, many of the worms raised their front ends and waved them from side to side. One out of twelve worms quickly darted into its burrow. After fifteen minutes, most worms had retreated back into the earth. When Darwin set a lamp next to the pots before nightfall, he discovered that the worms wouldn't show up at all, even when it got dark outside.

Another time, Darwin used a lens to concentrate light on the worms, and whammo, down they ducked in a flash. Only one worm out of seventy-two could stand it. Would worms act like this all the time? Darwin watched worms in many situations and later discovered that worms that were mating or feeding sometimes stayed outside their burrows for as long as an hour or two after daybreak.

As with most experiments, Darwin's light tests created as many questions as answers. Why did worms react differently to different colored light? Why did they wave their heads? Why did they sometimes ignore light while feeding or mating? Maybe you can discover the answers!

Sound Experiments

Perhaps Darwin's neighbors would have thought he was nuts if they had spied him testing worm hearing. What would you think if you saw someone making strange sounds to a pot of soil in a dimly lit room? Darwin watched his worms as he whistled, played the bassoon, and shouted. As far as he could see, none of this racket had any effect. When Darwin set the worm pots on a table right next to his piano and pounded away on the keys, they didn't dance, clap, or show any reaction.

What do you think happened when he put them on the piano while he played? Playing the C note in the bass clef sent them down under, and so did the G note. Yet some other notes had no effect. Worms can't hear as we do, but they are sensitive to vibrations. Do you wonder what worms do when a herd of kids plays tag on their rooftop?

Other Experiments

Darwin also did numerous experiments to judge the intelligence of worms. He watched how they solved the problem of dragging different-shaped leaves and paper into their burrows. Since they seemed to figure out the easiest way to pull in the leaves and paper, he concluded that they could learn by trial and error—by making mistakes and trying again until they got it right. Darwin also

examined how worms recycle natural waste and how they enrich the soil. After a lifetime of study, he was without a doubt an expert on worms. Yet his book is full of unanswered questions and puzzles for modern wormologists.

Darwin wasn't the only scientist to test worms' learning abilities. Many scientists have used mazes to discover if worms can learn to avoid nasty conditions. The most common type of maze used is a T maze, a T-shaped box. In 1912, R. M. Yerkes used a glass T maze with an open bottom that rested on wet paper. Worms entered through a hole at the bottom of the T. Once inside the maze, they had a choice of two different arms to wander into. In one arm Yerkes set up a strip of sandpaper and beyond that, two **electrodes** resting on a strip of rubber. The electrodes gave off a slight electrical jolt. The other arm was empty.

At first, the worms investigated both arms, but after running into the sandpaper and electrodes, they soon began to avoid that arm by turning into the safe one. Yerkes concluded that the worms learned to avoid the electrodes.

In 1957, another scientist, Jack Arbit, used a T maze for similar experiments, but tested at different times of the day. One batch of worms was tested between eight in the morning and noon, and the other between eight in the evening and midnight. The worms tested in the evening needed fewer tries before they began to stay away from the electrodes. Arbit concluded that a worm's ability to learn depends on the time of day it is most active.

In 1973 two other scientists who were conducting some experiments with trails of mucus wondered if worms in T mazes were really learning to avoid nasty experiences or if they were merely getting messages from worm slime. Perhaps after a bad experience, worms secrete a substance into their mucus that tells them which path they should take.

Learning from experience is regarded as a sign of basic intelligence, and mazes are often used by scientists for intelligence testing. Do you think worms can learn from experience? Can you set up experiments to test your ideas?

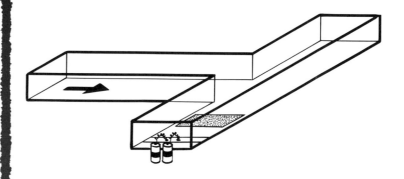

Even though many adult and kid scientists have studied worms, there are still many earthworm mysteries. One thing that many people, including Charles Darwin, have wondered is why earthworms leave their burrows after a heavy rain. Although it is known that worms can usually survive in water for long periods of time, some scientists think that the rainwater flooding their burrows is low in oxygen, and they are forced to surface for air. Others wonder if acids from carbon dioxide cause them to leave. Though people have been curious about rainy-day worms for a long time, it seems that more research is needed to prove exactly why they surface after a downpour.

Mysteries of a Backyard Buddy

Despite the fact that worms are seemingly simple backyard buddies, there is still a lot to learn about them. Most kids, like yourself, are pros when it comes to conjuring up questions that can't be answered by the teacher or textbook. Difficult questions are far more valuable to a scientist than easy answers. Scientific exploration is a never-ending adventure, since questions always lead to more questions. The kids in my town found lots of questions as they investigated earthworms. A few are listed below.

Do worms know where they are going?

Why are they so quiet?

Can earthworms be trained to jump or do other tricks?

How many colors do they come in?

Do worms have the same slime as slugs?

Did you run into any unsolved mysteries as you followed your questions?

Glossary

annelid: a worm with a long body divided into rings or segments. (Also called a segmented worm.)

burrow: an underground tunnel lined with worm slime

casting: worm manure

clitellum: a saddlelike structure which produces a cocoon for baby worms

cocoon: a protective covering often made of fibers

electrode: a device that collects or gives off electrical charges

hermaphrodite: an animal that posesses both male and female parts

intestines: part of the body where final food digestion takes place

invertebrates: animals that do not have backbones

mucus: a sticky substance that keeps skin moist

scavenger: an animal that searches around for discarded material

segmented worm: a worm with its body divided into ringlike sections

setae: bristlelike hairs on each segment of a worm, which are used for gripping

species: a group of animals with common traits, especially their ability to produce young

Index

About the Author

For the last twenty years, Michael Elsohn Ross has taught visitors to Yosemite National Park about the park's wildlife and geology. Michael, his wife, Lisa (a nurse who served nine seasons as a ranger-naturalist), and their son, Nick, have led other families on wilderness expeditions from the time Nick learned to crawl. Mr. Ross studied Conservation of Natural Resources at the University of California/Berkeley, with a minor in entomology (the study of insects). He spent one summer at Berkeley raising thousands of red-humped caterpillars and parasitic wasps for experiments.

Raised in Huntington, New York, Mr. Ross now makes his home on a bluff above the wild and scenic Merced River, at the entrance to Yosemite. His backyard garden is a haven for rolypolies, crickets, snails, slugs, worms, and a myriad of other intriguing critters.